Mad
aBouT
joKes

BEANObooks
geddes & grosset

Why is a polar bear cheap to have as a pet?
It lives on ice!

What's a teddy bear's favourite pasta?
Tagliateddy!

Why was the little bear so spoiled?
Because its mother panda'd to its every whim!

What do you get if you cross a grizzly bear and a harp?
A bear faced lyre!

What kind of money is used by polar bears?
Ice lolly!

BASH STREET KIDS

What is a bear's favourite drink?
Koka-Koala!

What do Alexander the Great and Winnie the Pooh have in common?
They both have 'the' as their middle names!

Why do bears have fur coats?
Because they'd look stupid in anoraks!

What do you get if you cross a teddy bear with a pig?
A teddy boar!

How do you tell a brown bear from a grizzly bear?
Answer 1: Climb a tree. If the bear climbs it and eats you, it's a brown bear.
Answer 2: If the bear knocks the tree down and eats you, it's a grizzly.

What do bees chew?
Bumble gum!

What bee is good for your health?
Vitamin bee!

Why did the queen bee throw out all of the other bees?
Because they kept droning on and on!

What's a bee-line?
The shortest distance between two buzz-stops!

What did the confused bee say?
To bee or not to bee!

What do you call a Russian flea?
A Moscow-ito!

What do you call an ant that likes to be alone?
An independant!

Why didn't the two worms get aboard Noah's Ark in an apple?
Because everyone had to go on in pairs (pears)!

What do you call a flea that lives in Smiffy's ear?
A space invader!

How can you tell which end of a worm is which?
Tickle it in the middle and see which end laughs!

What is the difference between a flea and a wolf?
One prowls on the hairy and the other howls on the prairie!

What kind of bee can't be understood?
A mumble bee!

How do you find where a flea has bitten you?
Start from scratch!

What's life like for a wood worm?
Boring!

What insect runs away from everything?
A flee!

THE BURRD

THAT PLANE REFUELLING THE SMALLER ONE REMINDS ME.

IT'S TIME I REFUELLED YOUNG JOEY.

What's black, yellow and covered in blackberries?
A bramble bee!

How do fleas travel?
Itch hiking!

What do you get if you cross a worm and an elephant?
Enormous worm holes in your garden!

When is the best time to buy budgies?
When they're going cheap!

How does a bird with a broken wing manage to land safely?
With its sparrowchute!

What is a parrot's favourite game?
Hide and Speak!

What do you call a woodpecker with no beak?
A headbanger!

What do you get if you cross a parrot with a shark?
A bird that will talk your ear off!

What do you get if you cross a parrot with a woodpecker?
A bird that talks in morse code!

THE BURRD

What's got six legs and can fly long distances?
Three swallows !

What do baby swans dance to?
Cygnet-ure-tunes!

What happens when ducks fly upside down?
They quack up!

How do you know that owls are cleverer than chickens?
Have you ever heard of Kentucky-fried owl?

CALAMITY JAMES

BOY: "Dad, Dad! There's a monster at the door with a really ugly face!"
DAD: "Tell him you've already got one!"

Did you hear about the little boy who was named after his father?
They called him Dad!

Why was the boy unhappy to win the prize for the best costume at the Halloween party?
Because he'd just come along to pick up his little sister!

A boy went to a Halloween party with a sheet over his head.
"Are you here as a ghost?" asked his friends.
"No, I'm an unmade bed."
Another boy arrived with a sheet over his head.
"Have you come as an unmade bed, too?" asked his friends.
"No, I'm an undercover agent," he replied.

Dennis is the type of boy that his mother doesn't want him to associate with!

Dennis and Gnasher went into a modern art gallery by mistake.
"Quick, Gnasher, run," cried Dennis looking at one of the exhibits. "Before they say **we** did it!"

YOUNG SID THE COPPER'S KID

DAD! THERE'S A NASTY MAN WITH A BALL AND CHAIN ROUND THE CORNER.

THAT'LL BE CONVICT CONRAD!

WOW! IT'S JEFF THE REF. HE'S EVEN MORE UNPOPULAR.

A little boy went into a baker's. "How much are those cream cakes?" he asked.

"Two for 75p," replied the baker.

"How much does one cost?" asked the boy.

"38p," said the baker.

"Then I'll take the other one for 37p!" said the boy.

A boy with a newt on his shoulder walked into a library.

"What do you call him?" asked the librarian.

"Tiny," answered the boy.

"Why did you decide to call him Tiny?"

"Because he's 'my newt'!"

MUM: "Haven't you finished filling the salt shaker yet?"

SMIFFY: "Not yet. It's really hard getting the salt through all those little holes!"

YOUNG SID THE COPPER'S KID

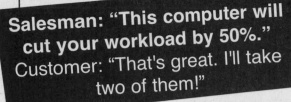

Salesman: "This computer will cut your workload by 50%."
Customer: "That's great. I'll take two of them!"

Computer Helpline
"Every time I log on to the seven dwarfs website, my computer screen goes snow white...."

"Doctor, doctor, I think I'm part of the Internet!"
"Well, you do look a site!"

Computer Helpline
"I've just pushed a piece of bacon into my disk drive!"
"Has the computer stopped working?"
"No, but there's a lot of crackling."

"If you don't stop tapping away at that keyboard I think I'll go crazy."
"I think you already have! I stopped using the keyboard over an hour ago."

Customer: "This computer you charged me £950 for doesn't work....and you said it would be trouble free."
Shop Assistant: "It is. I charged you £950 for the computer, but you're getting all that trouble absolutely free!"

What did the blue keyboard say to the green keyboard?
Sorry, you're not my type.

"Doctor, doctor, I've spent so long at my PC, I've got double vision."
"Well, try going around with one eye shut."

What do you get if you cross a computer with a ballet dancer?
The Netcracker Suite!

"Doctor, doctor, I think I'm a computer!"
"How long have you felt like this?"
"Ever since I was switched on!"

What do you get if you type www.abcdefghijklmnopqrst uvwxyz.com into your computer?
A sore finger!

When do computers go to sleep?
When it's internight.

How do bank robbers send messages?
By flee mail!

"Doctor, doctor, I don't think I'm a computer anymore. Now I think I'm a desk."
"Don't let things get on top of you."

Why did the ape log on to the Internet?
To send a chimpanzee-mail.

Who holds up stagecoaches and steals lap-top computers?
Click Turpin!

"Would you like to buy a second-hand computer?"
"Not likely! I find it hard enough to type with one hand as it is."

First internit: "Why are you looking so worried?"

Second internit: "Last night I sent myself an anonymous e-mail and now I don't know who it's from."

Why do computer tutors never get sick?
Because an 'apple' a day keeps the doctor away.

Why did the duck stick his leg into a computer?
He wanted to have webbed feet.

How do dolphins send messages?
By sea-mail!

Writer: "I've been typing on the Internet so much, my right hand's begun to ache."
Doctor: "That's just age."
Writer: "But my left hand is just as old and it doesn't ache at all."

Minnie: "Sir, would you mind e-mailing my exam results to my parents?"
Teacher: "But your parents don't have a computer."
Minnie: "Exactly!"

DESPERATE DAN

What happened when the lion ate the comedian?
He felt funny!

What does a lion brush his mane with?
A catacomb!

What do you get if you cross a tiger with a kangaroo?
A stripy jumper!

What do you get if you cross a tiger with a snowman?
Frostbite!

What is a French cat's favourite pudding?
Chocolate mousse!

What looks like half a cat?
The other half!

If a four-legged animal is a quadruped and a two-legged animal is a biped, what's a tiger?
A stri-ped!

DENNIS THE MENACE

What is a ghost's favourite dessert?
Boo-berry pie and I-scream!

What is Count Dracula's favourite snack?
A fangfurter!

Who brings the monsters their babies?
Frankenstork!

When do ghosts usually appear?
Just before someone screams!

What noise does a witch's breakfast cereal make?
Snap, cackle and pop!

How does a monster count to 21?
On his fingers!

What happened to the monster that took the five o'clock train home?
He had to give it back.

How do vampire footballers get the mud off?
They all get in the bat tub!

Why was the werewolf arrested in the butcher's shop?
He was found chop-lifting!

What do witches put in their hair?
Scare spray!

What's a ghoul's favourite breakfast cereal?
Rice Creepies!

What do spooks mail home while on holiday?
Ghostcards.

What does a sorceress wear?
A bewitching outfit.

Where can you see a real ugly monster?
In the mirror.

What do you call a monster with no neck?
The Lost Neck Monster.

What's Dracula's favourite dance?
The fang-dango.

What do you call a ghost's mother and father?
Transparents!

What do you call a black cat that can spring up a six foot wall?
A good jumpurr!

Why did the ghost cross the road?
To get to 'THE OTHER SIDE'!

What should you say when you meet a ghost?
How do you boo!

What do you get when dinosaurs crash their cars?
Tyrannosaurus wrecks!

Why do dinosaurs wear glasses?
To make sure they don't step on other dinosaurs.

How can you tell a male dinosaur from a female dinosaur?
Ask it a question. If HE answers, it's a male and if SHE answers, it's female!

What do you call a fossil that doesn't want to work?
Lazy bones!

What do you get if you cross a pig with a dinosaur?
Jurassic Pork!

What did the dinosaur say after the accident?
I'msosaurus

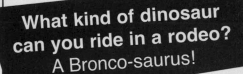

What kind of dinosaur can you ride in a rodeo?
A Bronco-saurus!

What do you call it when a dinosaur makes a goal with a football?
A dino-score!

What do you get when you cross a dinosaur with fireworks?
DINOMITE!

Why did the dinosaur walk on two legs?
To give the ants a chance!

What do you call a sleeping plated dinosaur?
Stegosnorus!

What do you call a tyrannosaurus that talks and talks and talks ...?
A dinobore!

What was the scariest prehistoric animal?
The Terror-dactyl!

Why did the dinosaur cross the road?
The chicken hadn't evolved yet!

What did the Tyrannosaurus rex get after exercising at the gym?
Dino-sore!

What made the dinosaur's car stop?
A flat Tire-annosaurus.

What do you call Tyrannosaurus rex when it wears a cowboy hat and boots?
Tyrannosaurus tex!

What do you call a dinosaur that never gives up?
Try-try-try-ceratops!

What do you get if you cross a Triceratops with a kangaroo?
A Tricera-hops!

DINAH MO

"Doctor, Doctor, some days I feel like a tee-pee and other days I feel like a wig-wam."
"Relax. You're too tents."

"Doctor, Doctor, I feel like biscuits!"
"What, you mean those square ones?"
"Yes!"
"The ones you put butter on?"
"Yes!"
"You're crackers!"

"Doctor, Doctor, my little boy has just swallowed a roll of film!"
"Hmmmm. Let's hope nothing develops."

"Doctor, Doctor, you have to help me out!"
"No problem, which way did you come in?"

"Doctor, Doctor, I keep getting a pain in the eye when I drink coffee."
"Have you tried taking the spoon out of your cup?"

"Doctor, Doctor, my sister thinks she is a lift."
"Well, tell her to come in and see me."
"I can't, she doesn't stop at this floor!"

Smiffy: "Doctor, Doctor, what did the x-ray of my head show?"
Doctor: "Absolutely nothing, I'm afraid!"

"Doctor, Doctor, everyone thinks I'm a liar."
"Oh, I can't believe that!"

"Doctor, Doctor, I snore so loudly at night I keep myself awake."
"Sleep in another room then!"

"Doctor, Doctor, I swallowed a bone!"
"Are you choking?"
"No, I really did!"

Doctor: "You seem to be in excellent health. Your pulse is as regular as clockwork."
Patient: "That's because you've got your hand on my watch!"

Why do elephants float down the river on their backs?
So they won't get their tennis shoes wet!

What is the difference between an Indian and an African elephant?
About three thousand miles.

Why do elephants have cracks between their toes?
For carrying their library cards.

What's the difference between eating an elephant and eating peanut butter?
Elephants don't stick to the roof of your mouth!

What is big, grey and wears glass slippers?
Cinderellaphant!

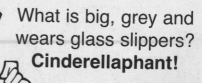

What do you call an elephant taking a bite out of the computer?
A mega-byte!

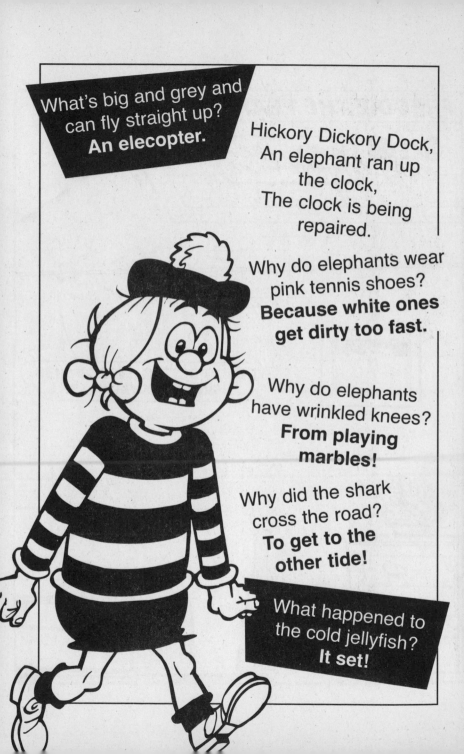

Where do little fishes go every morning?
To 'plaice' school!

Why are sardines the stupidest fish in the sea?
Because they climb into tins, close the lid and leave the key outside!

What's the coldest fish in the sea?
The blue whale!

Where would seaweed look for a job?
In the 'Kelp-wanted' ads!

Why are dolphins cleverer than humans?
They can train a man to stand at the side of a pool and feed them fish!

Who held the baby octopus to ransom?
Squidnappers!

What fish do road-workers use?
Pneumatic krill!

What do you call a fish with no eyes?
Fsh!

Where are most fish found? Between the head and the tail!

What do you get if you cross a trout with an apartment? A flat fish!

How many frogs does it take to screw in a light bulb? **One frog and 37 light bulbs. Frogs have slippery hands!**

What kind of shoes do frogs wear? **Open toad!**

What did the frog order at McDonald's? **French flies and a diet Croak!**

What's green, green, green, green, green? **A frog rolling down a hill.**

Why did the frog make so many mistakes? **It jumped to the wrong conclusions.**

What is a frog's favourite snack? **Cheese and croakers.**

What do you get if you cross a frog with a ferry?
A hoppercraft !

What do you get if cross a science fiction film with a toad?
Star Warts!

Why did the tadpole feel lonely?
Because he was newt to the area!

How does a frog feel when he has a broken leg?
Unhoppy!

What did the frog say when he was given a book?
Reddit!

What part of a football pitch smells nicest?
The scenter spot!

Which team's goal keeper can jump higher than a crossbar?
All of them, a crossbar can't jump!

Manager: "I'll give you a hundred pounds a week to start with and two hundred pounds a week in a year's time!"
Young player: "OK, I'll come back in a year's time!"

IVY THE TERRIBLE

What's the chilliest ground in the premiership?
Cold Trafford!

What tea do footballers drink?
Penaltea!

If you have a referee in football, what do you have in bowls?
Cornflakes!

What stories are told by basketball players?
Tall stories!

Why did the chicken get sent off?
For persistent 'fowling'!

Which football team loves ice-cream?
Aston Vanilla!

How do hens encourage their football teams?
They egg them on!

How do you stop squirrels playing football in the garden?
Hide the ball. It drives them nuts!

IVY THE TERRIBLE

Why does a marathon runner make a good student? **Because education pays off in the long run!**

What is a runner's favourite subject in school? **Jog-raphy!**

Where do football directors go when they are fed up? **The bored room!**

What part of a football ground is never the same? **The changing rooms!**

Did you hear about the football team who ate too much pudding? **They were jellygated!**

Why do grasshoppers not go to many football matches?
They prefer cricket!

Referee: "I'm sending you off!"
Player: "What for?"
Referee: "The rest of the match!"

What is a goal keeper's favourite snack?
Beans on post!

Manager: "Our new midfielder cost fifteen million. I call him our wonder player!"
Fan: "Why's that?"
Manager: "Because everytime he plays, I wonder why I bought him!"

Minnie: "Do you like me?"
Dennis: "As girls go, you're okay and the sooner you go the better!"

"Now remember, Ivy," said the teacher. "You can tell a tree's age by counting the rings in a cross section. One ring for each year." When Ivy arrived home from school she found a chocolate roll on the table.
"I'm not eating that,"she told her mum. "It's five years old!"

"What did the boy Eskimo say to the girl Eskimo?"
"What's an ice girl like you doing in a place like this?"

Two girls were talking in the school corridor.
"That boy over there is getting on my nerves," said Laura.
"But he's not even looking at you," replied Lara.
"That's what's getting on my nerves," answered Laura.

"You never get anything right," complained Minnie's teacher.
"What kind of job do you think you'll get when you leave school?"
"Well, I want to be the weather girl on TV," replied Minnie.

"Excuse me," said Minnie, returning to her seat at the cinema, "but did I step on your toe as I went out?"
"You certainly did," the girl replied.
"Oh, good," said Minnie, "that means I'm in the right row!"

First girl: "Whenever I'm down in the dumps I buy myself a new outfit."
Second girl: "Oh, so that's where you get them."

Belinda: "James told me last night that he'd met the most beautiful girl in the world."
Barbara: "Oh, dear, I'm sorry. I thought he was going to marry YOU!"

Did you hear about the girl who was so careful about road safety that she always wore white at night? **Last winter she was knocked down by a snow plough!**

Minnie's dad burst into the baker's shop and said: "I sent my daughter in for a kilo of biscuits this morning, but when I weighed them there was only half a kilo. I suggest you check your scales." **"No, sir," the baker replied, "I suggest you weigh your daughter!"**

Why didn't the dog speak to his foot? **Because it's not polite to talk back to your paw!**

What do you do if your dog eats your pen? **Use a pencil instead!**

What do you get if you cross a dog with Concorde? **A jet setter!**

THE DIRECTOR Menace.

When is the most likely time that a stray dog will walk into your house? **When the door is open!**

What do you get if you take a really big dog out for a walk? **A Great Dane out!**

What is a dog's favourite food? **Anything that's on your plate!**

What happened when the dog went to the flea circus? It stole the show!

Why is a dog's nose in the middle of it's face? Because it's the scenter.

Why do dogs wag their tails?
No one else will do it for them.

What is a dog's favourite joke?
Eating something really disgusting then licking your face.

What's the best way to prevent catching diseases caused by biting dogs?
Don't bite any dogs!

Why is it better to be a grasshopper than a cricket?
Because grasshoppers can play cricket but crickets can't play grasshopper!

What do you get if you cross a dog and a cheetah?
A dog that chases cars - and catches them!

LITTLE PLUM

OOH-WOO-WOO-WOO!

WHY YOU DO UM WAR DANCE, PLUM?

YOU'D DO ONE AS WELL IF A COLONY OF ANTS WERE MARCHING UNDER YOUR FEET.

What do bees do if they want to use public transport?
Wait at a buzz stop!

How do you know if you've been bitten by a tough mosquito?
You slap him and he slaps you back!

Where do ants go on their holidays?
Frants!

What did the worm say to the other when it was late home?
Where in earth have you been?

What goes hum-choo, hum-choo?
A bee with a cold!

What's the difference between a worm and an apple?
Have you ever tasted worm pie?!

MINNIE MINX

What did one firefly say to the other?
Got to glow now!

What do you call an ant that skips school?
A truant!

What do you get if you cross a centipede and a parrot?
A walkie talkie!

When should you stop for a glow worm?
When he has a red light!

Where would you put an injured insect?
In an antbulance!

What did the romantic flea say?
I love you aw-flea!

Which insect didn't play well in goal?
The fumble bee!

Why are glow worms good to carry in your bag?
They can lighten your load!

Why don't anteaters get sick?
Because they are full of antibodies!

What did the bumble bee striker say?
Hive scored!

How can you tell if you are looking at a police glow worm?
It has a blue light!

What story do little witches like to hear at bedtime?
Ghoul deluxe and the three scares!

Who comes to a witch's wedding?
The bride and broom.

MUTT 'N' MOGGY

Was Dracula ever married?
No, he was a bat-chelor!

What do you call a wizard from outer space?
A flying sorcerer!

Where do ghosts go on holiday?
The Ghosta Brava!

What is a devil's picket line called?
A **demon**stration!

Why do demons and ghouls get on so well?
Because demons are a ghouls best friend!

How do you get the most apples when bobbing at Halloween?
Wear a snorkel!

Why are black cats such good singers?
They're very **mew**sical!

Why did the boy carry a clock and a bird on Halloween?
It was for "tick or tweet"!

What do ghosts say when a girl footballer is sent off?
Ban-she, ban-she!

First Witch: "My, hasn't your little girl grown?"
Second witch: "Yes, she's certainly gruesome."

First Monster: "That gorgeous ghoul over there just rolled her eyes at me."
Second Monster: "Well you'd better roll them back to her, she might need them."

What happened to the girl who wore a mouse costume to the Hallowe'en party?
The cat ate her!

Boy Monster: "You've got a face like a million dollars."
Girl Monster: "Have I really?"
Boy Monster: "Yes, its green and wrinkly!"

What happened when the wizard turned a naughty boy into a hare?
Oh, he's still rabbiting on about it!

Why did the small werewolf bite the girl's ankle?
Because he couldn't reach any higher!

Minnie: "Are you having a party for your birthday?"
Ivy: No, I'm having a witch do."
Minnie: "What's a witch do?"
Ivy: "She flies around on a broomstick casting spells."

Why did the boy take a pain killer after hearing a werewolf howl?
Because it gave him an eerie ache!

Teacher: "I'd like you to be very quiet today, girls. I've got a terrible headache."

Minnie: "Please, miss! Why don't you do what my mum does when she has a headache?"

Teacher: "What's that?"

Minnie: "She sends us out to play!"

An Eskimo teacher was reciting the nursery rhyme Little Jack Horner to her class of five-year-olds. She got as far as 'Little Jack Horner sat in the corner' when one of the children put up her hand and said, "Please, miss, what's a corner?"

Teacher: "Can you give me three reasons why the world is round."

Smiffy: "Well, my dad says so, my mum says so and you say so!"

Teacher: "Who was the first woman on earth?"

Smiffy: "I don't know, sir."

Teacher: "Come on, it has something to do with an apple."

Smiffy: "Granny Smith?"

Father: "I want to take my daughter out of this terrible maths class."
Teacher: "But she's top of the class."
Father: "That's why I think it must be a terrible class."

"Miss Smith says that I've got such bad handwriting that I ought to be a doctor!"

"I hope you're not one of those boys who sits and watches the school clock," said the school principal to a new boy.
"No, sir. I've got a digital watch that bleeps at half past three."

When the English teacher asked her class to write an essay on what they'd do if they had a million dollars, Minnie handed in a blank sheet of paper.
"Minnie!" yelled the teacher, "You've done nothing! Why?"
"Because if I had a million dollars, that's exactly what I would do!"

Pupil: "I don't think I deserved the 0% you gave me for that test."
Teacher: "Neither do I, but it's the lowest mark I could give!"

Teacher : "Minnie, put some more water in the fish tank!"
Minnie: "Why, miss? I only put some in yesterday and they haven't drunk that yet!"

Mum: "Why does your maths test have a big zero over it?"
Minnie: "It's not a zero. The teacher ran out of stars, so she gave me a moon instead!"

Teacher : "What are you reading?"
Pupil : "I dunno, sir!"
Teacher : "But you're reading aloud!"
Pupil : "But I'm not listening!"

Dad: "What did you learn in school today, Ivy?"
Ivy: "That three and three are seven."
Dad: "Three and three are six!"
Ivy: "Then it looks like I didn't learn anything today!"

Boy: "Here's my report!"
Dad: "Well there's one thing in your favour, son, with grades like this you can't be cheating!"

Teacher: "Why are you the only child in the classroom today?"
Plug: "Because I was the only one who didn't have school dinners yesterday!"

Minnie: "Are you in the top half of your class?"
Dennis: "No, I'm one of the students who makes the top half possible!"

Teacher: "Smith, didn't you hear me call you?"
Smith: "Yes, sir, but you told us not to answer back!"

Teacher: "You missed school yesterday, didn't you?"
Minnie: "Not a bit!"

Teacher: "What do we call the outer skin of a tree?"
Smiffy: "Don't know, miss!"
Teacher: "Bark, silly, bark!"
Smiffy: "Woof, woof!"

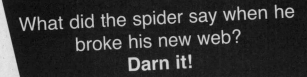

What did the spider say when he
broke his new web?
Darn it!

What did the spider say to the fly?
**We're getting married - do you
want to come to the webbing?**

Why are spiders like tops?
They are always spinning!

What are spiders' webs
good for?
Spiders!

STRANGE HILL SCHOOL

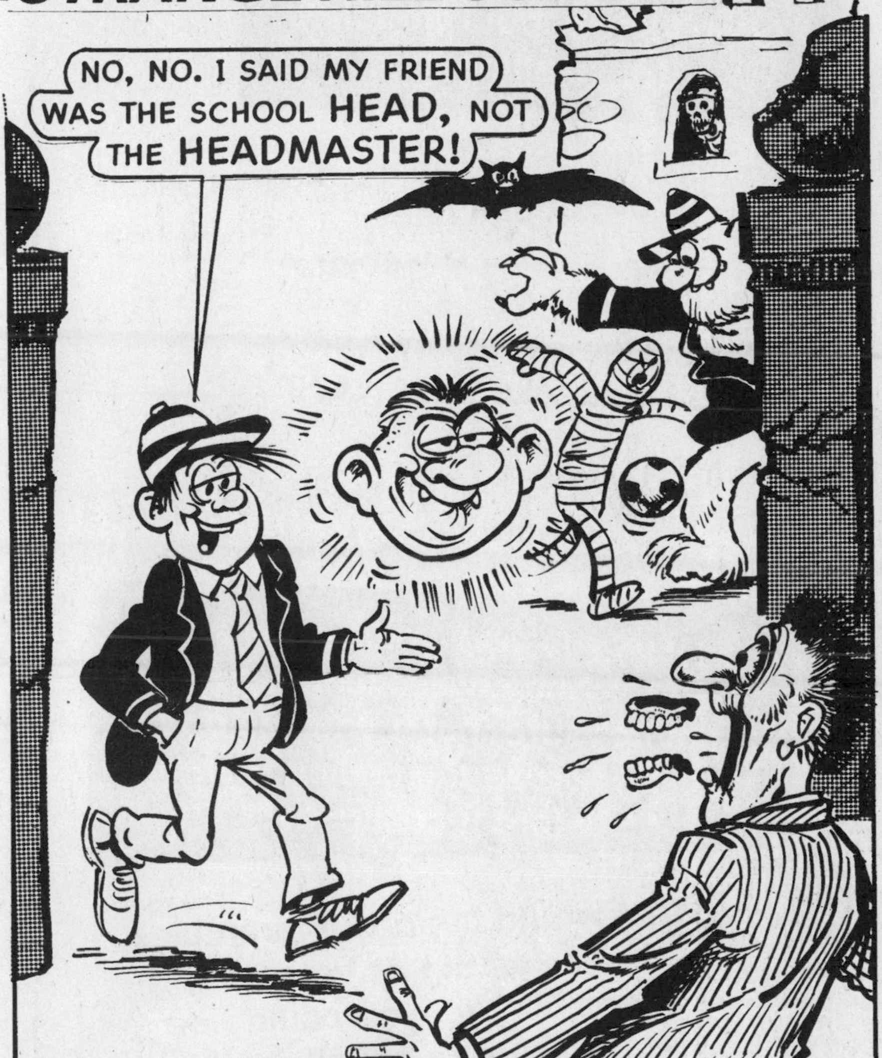

What do you get if you cross a tarantula with a rose?
I don't know, but I wouldn't try smelling it!

How do you spot a modern spider?
He doesn't have a web he has a website!

Why did the spider buy a car?
So he could take it for a spin!

What do you call a 100 spiders on a tyre?
A spinning wheel!

What do you get if you cross a spider and an elephant?
I'm not sure, but if you see one walking across the ceiling then run before it collapses!

**What would happen if tarantulas were as big as horses?
If one bit you, you could ride it to hospital!**

Where did the pilgrims land
when they came to
America?
On their feet!

**Did Native Americans
hunt bear?**
Not in the winter!

Minnie: If Spanish explorers went
round the world in a galleon,
how many galleons did they get to
the mile?

What did Noah do while
spending time on the ark?
He fished. He didn't catch
much, though, he only had
two worms!

**Who invented King
Arthur's round
table?**
Sir Circumference!

What did
Napoleon become
when he was 41
years old?
A year older!

WALTER THE SOFTY

Smiffy: Wish I had been born 1000 years ago.
Minnie: Why is that?
Smiffy: Just think of all the history that I wouldn't have to learn!

What famous chiropodist ruled England?
William the Corn-cutter!

What was the first thing Queen Elizabeth did on ascending to the throne?
She sat down!

What did the Sheriff of Nottingham say when Robin Hood fired at him?
That was an arrow escape!